HAL•LEONARD

BASS PLAY•ALONG™

VOL. 48

JAMES BROWN

T0057506

Cover photo: Michael Ochs Archives/Getty Images

ISBN 978-1-4803-3238-6

HAL•LEONARD®
CORPORATION

7777 W. BLUEMOUND RD. P.O. BOX 13819 MILWAUKEE, WI 53213

Visit Hal Leonard Online at
www.halleonard.com

CONTENTS

Bass Notation Legend

Bass music can be notated two different ways: on a *musical staff*, and in *tablature*

THE MUSICAL STAFF shows pitches and rhythms and is divided by bar lines into measures. Pitches are named after the first seven letters of the alphabet.

TABLATURE graphically represents the bass fingerboard. Each horizontal line represents a string, and each number represents a fret.

Notes:

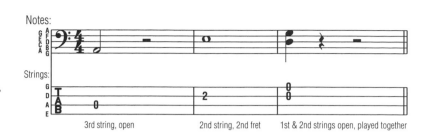

3rd string, open   2nd string, 2nd fret   1st & 2nd strings open, played together

HAMMER-ON: Strike the first (lower) note with one finger, then sound the higher note (on the same string) with another finger by fretting it without picking.

PULL-OFF: Place both fingers on the notes to be sounded. Strike the first note and without picking, pull the finger off to sound the second (lower) note.

LEGATO SLIDE: Strike the first note and then slide the same fret-hand finger up or down to the second note. The second note is not struck.

SHIFT SLIDE: Same as legato slide, except the second note is struck.

TRILL: Very rapidly alternate between the notes indicated by continuously hammering on and pulling off.

TREMOLO PICKING: The note is picked as rapidly and continuously as possible.

VIBRATO: The string is vibrated by rapidly bending and releasing the note with the fretting hand.

SHAKE: Using one finger, rapidly alternate between two notes on one string by sliding either a half-step above or below.

NATURAL HARMONIC: Strike the note while the fret hand lightly touches the string directly over the fret indicated.

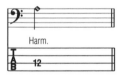

MUFFLED STRINGS: A percussive sound is produced by laying the fret hand across the string(s) without depressing them and striking them with the pick hand.

BEND: Strike the note and bend up the interval shown.

BEND AND RELEASE: Strike the note and bend up as indicated, then release back to the original note. Only the first note is struck.

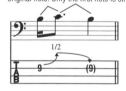

RIGHT-HAND TAP: Hammer ("tap") the fret indicated with the "pick-hand" index or middle finger and pull off to the note fretted by the fret hand.

LEFT-HAND TAP: Hammer ("tap") the fret indicated with the "fret-hand" index or middle finger.

SLAP: Strike ("slap") string with right-hand thumb.

POP: Snap ("pop") string with right-hand index or middle finger.

Additional Musical Definitions

 (accent)
- Accentuate note (play it louder)

 (accent)
- Accentuate note with great intensity

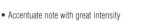 *(staccato)*
- Play the note short

D.S. al Coda
- Go back to the sign (𝄋), then play until the measure marked ***"To Coda"***, then skip to the section labelled ***"Coda."***

Fill
- Label used to identify a brief pattern which is to be inserted into the arrangement.

- Repeat measures between signs.

- When a repeated section has different endings, play the first ending only the first time and the second ending only the second time.

Call Me Super Bad (Parts 1, 2 & 3)

Words and Music by James Brown

Intro
Moderately fast ♩ = 126

*Chord symbols reflect overall harmony.

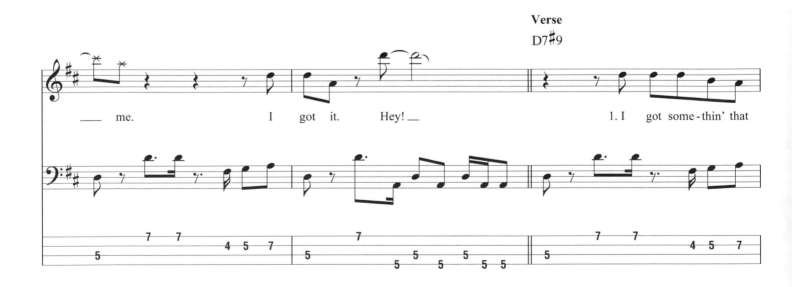

tells me what to do. __ Some-times I see it. Ha. Now,

I got __ a move __ that tells me what to do. __ Some-times I feel so nice, __ I

wan-na try my-self a few, __ ha. Ha. I got soul, _____ and I'm su-per bad. __

__ Ha. 3. I __ love, __ uh, I

Verse

D7#9

I said I'm su-per bad. __ Bridge! Come on. __

Bridge

G7

Up and down, and 'round and __ 'round.

Up and down, all __

__ a - round. __ Right on, peo - ple, ha,

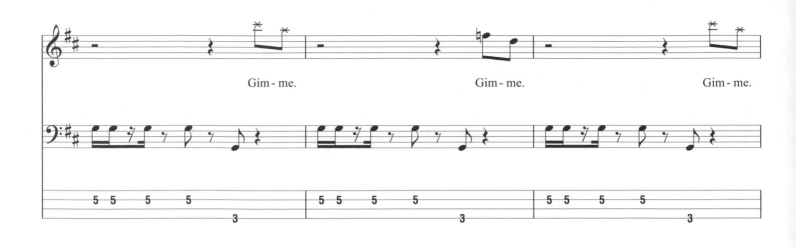

Gim - me.　　　　Gim - me.　　　　Gim - me.

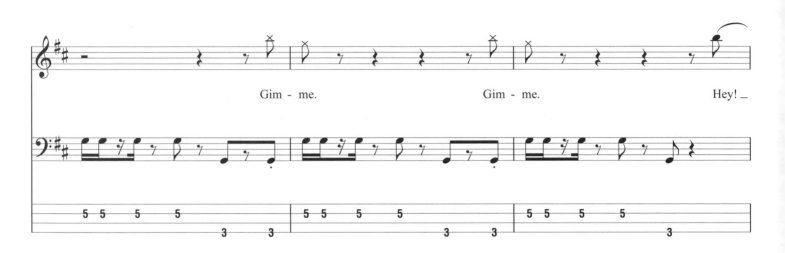

Gim - me.　　　　Gim - me.　　　　Hey! __

Interlude

A7　　　　D7#9

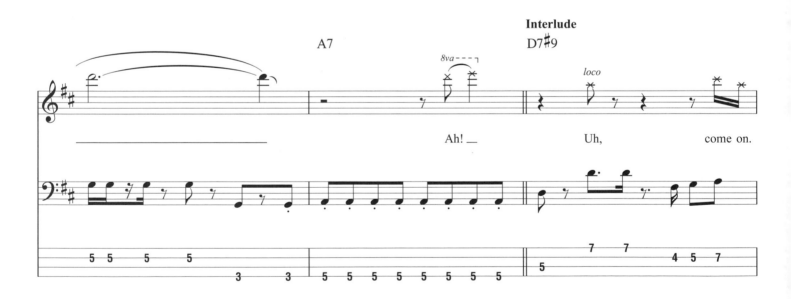

Ah! __　　　　Uh,　　come on.

Verse

D7#9

4. I got the some - thing   that makes me wan - na shout. __

I got the thing __ to tell __ me what it's all a - bout, _ uh.

I got __ soul, _____ ha,   and I'm su - per bad. _____   Heh.

you won't know, _ a, what it's all __ a - bout. _

_

Gim - me. Gim - me.

Gim - me. Gim-

me. Ah. _____

A7

Uh. Gim - me.

Gim - me. I said I'm su-per bad. __

Uh, su - per bad,

broth - er, ha, heh. Su-per bad, _____ uh.

Come on, __ Phelps.　　Come on.　　Su - per __

__ bad. __　　Jab, __ uh.　　Good

God.　　Su - per bad. _____　　Boot -

Begin fade　　　　　　　　　　　　　　　　*Fade out*

- sy,　huh,　　let me　hear ya.　　Su - per bad. _____

Cold Sweat, Pt. 1

Words and Music by James Brown and Alfred James Ellis

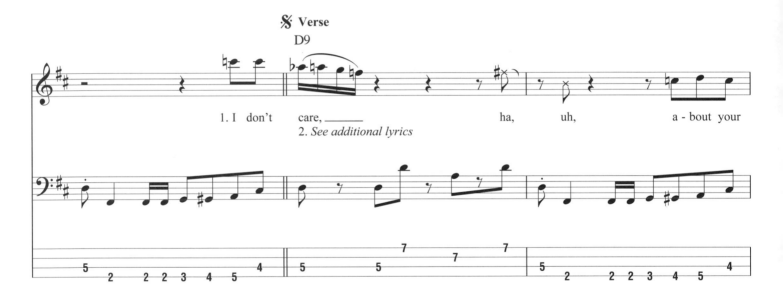

put it where it's at now.

Begin fade

Ah. _____ Let 'em have _ it.

Fade out

Uh!

Additional Lyrics

2. I don't care about your wants.
   I just wanna, ha, tell you 'bout your do's and don'ts.
   I don't care about the way you treat me, darlin'. Ha!
   I just want, ha, you understand me, honey. Oh!

Chorus When ya kiss me, no, and ya miss me.
   You hold me tight.
   Make ev'rything alright.
   I break out in a cold sweat. Ha.

Get Up Offa That Thing

Words and Music by Deanna Brown, Deidra Brown and Yamma Brown

Chorus

Get up off - a that thing. Fol - low me. Help me.

Get up off - a that thing, and dance till you ___ feel bet - ter.

Get up off - a that thing, and try to re - lease ___ that... Wait a min - ute!

Interlude

G7#9

The funk. So funk - y.

D7#9

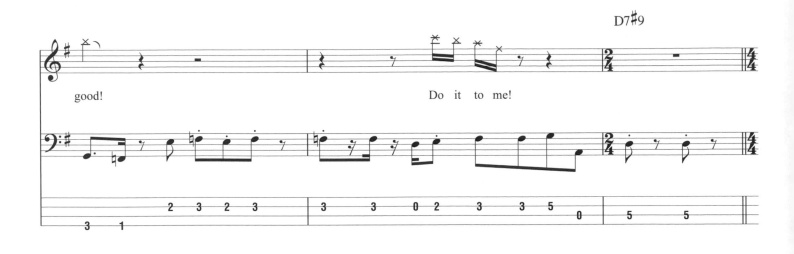

good!   Do it to me!

Outro-Chorus

G7#9

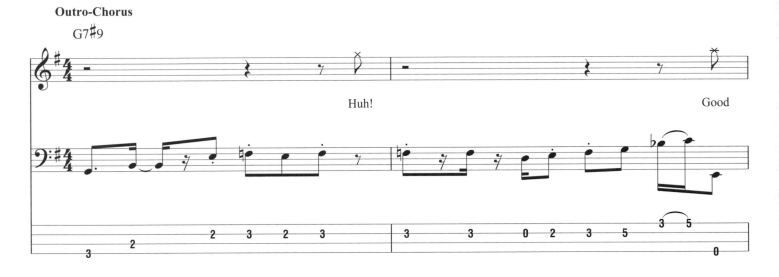

Huh!   Good

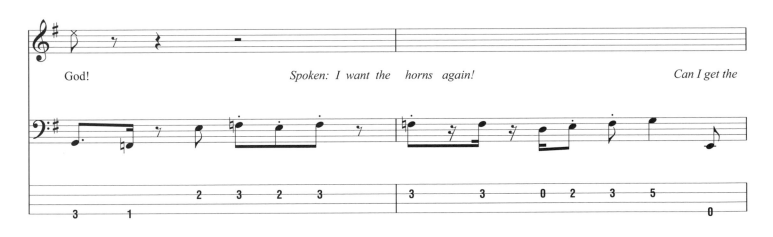

God!   *Spoken: I want the   horns again!*   *Can I get the*

horns again?   *Play that bad   funk!*   *Show 'em how funky you are!*

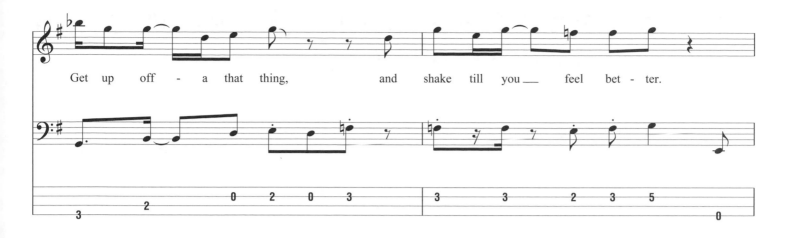

Get up off - a that thing, and shake till you __ feel bet - ter.

Get up off - a that thing, and try to re - lease __ that pres - sure.

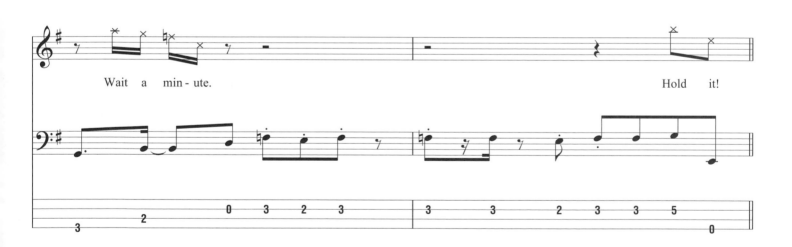

Wait a min - ute. Hold it!

Repeat and fade

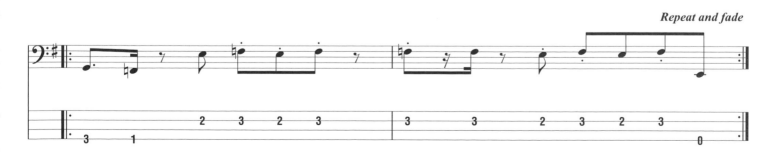

Get Up (I Feel Like Being) A Sex Machine

Words and Music by James Brown, Bobby Byrd and Ronald Lenhoff

Verse

Wait __ a min-ute. *(Get on up.)* 1. Shake your arm, __ then use __

__ your form. __ Stay on the scene, __ a, like a

sex ma-chine. ___ You got to have the feel-in',

sure as you're born. ___ Get __ it to-geth - er, right on, __

Chorus

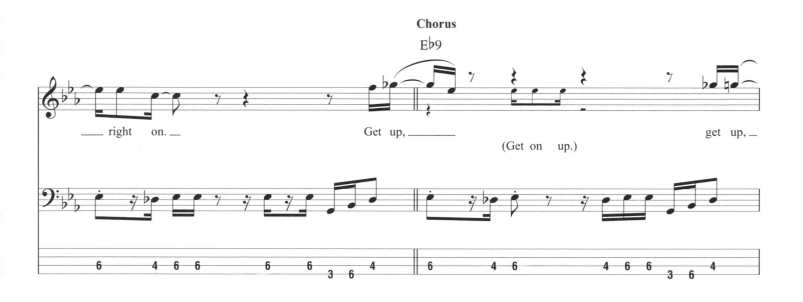

right on. Get up, Get up, get up,

(Get on up.)

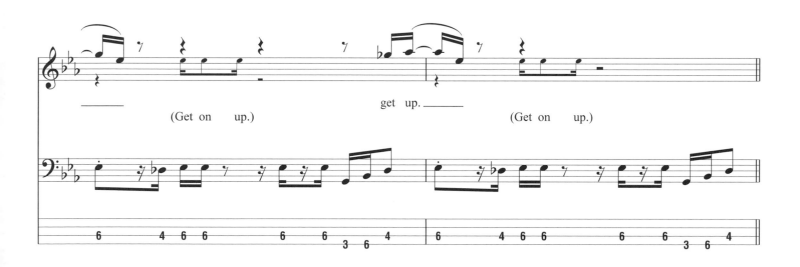

(Get on up.) get up. (Get on up.)

Interlude

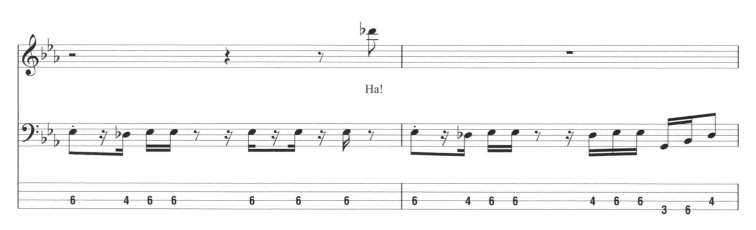

Ha!

Get up, ___

Chorus

E♭9

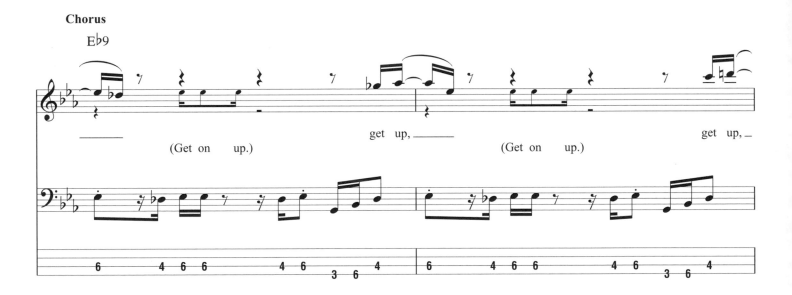

___ (Get on up.)   get up, ___   (Get on up.)   get up, ___

___ (Get on up.)   get up. ___   (Get on up.)   2. You said, ___

Verse

Eb9

you said you got to.   You said the

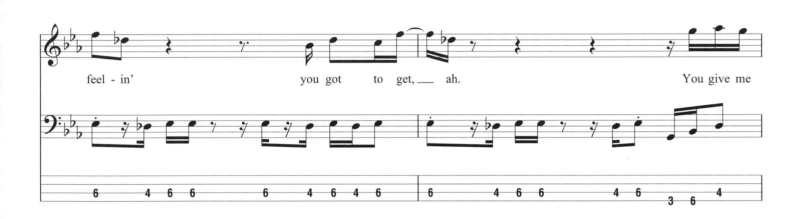

feel - in'   you got to get, __ ah.   You give me

fe - ver   in a cold sweat. __   The

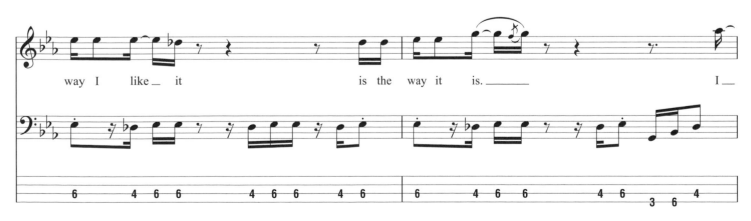

way I like __ it   is the way it is. _____   I __

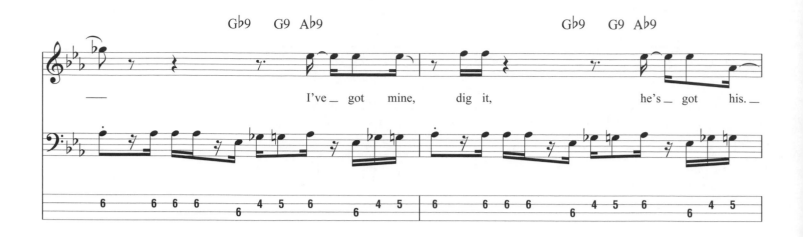

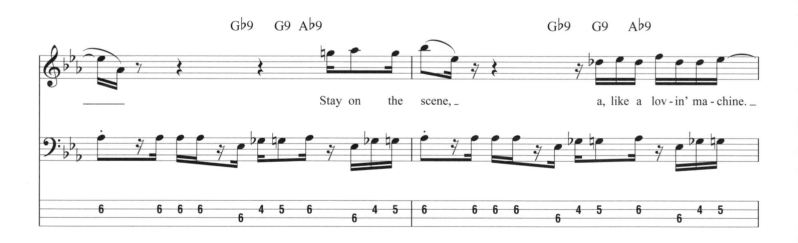

scene,   a, like a lov - in' ma - chine, __ ah.   Get up, __

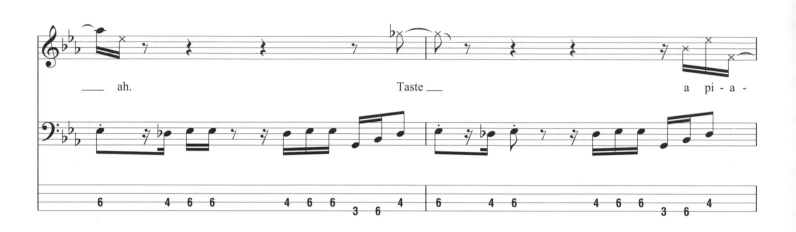

__ ah.   Taste __   a pi - a -

- na.   Taste __   a pi - a -

Interlude

E♭9

Play 7 times

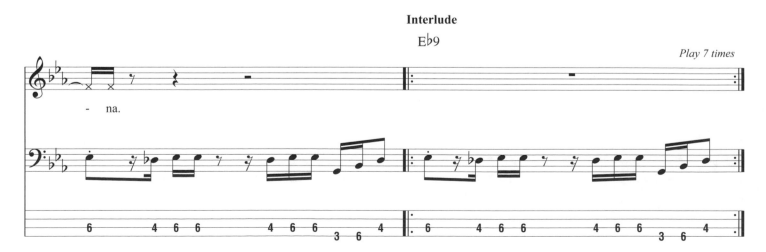

- na.

Chorus

Bkgd. Voc.: w/ Voc. Fig. 1 (6 times)

Get up, ___ ah. Get up, ___

___ ah. Stay on the scene a, like a sex ma - chine, ___

___ ah. You got - ta have the feel - in' sure as you're born. ___

Get it ___ to - geth - er, right on, ___

Shake your mon - ey mak - er. Shake your mon - ey mak - er.

Shake your mon - ey mak - er. Shake your mon - ey mak - er.

Chorus

Bkgd. Voc.: w/ Voc. Fig. 1 (5 times)

Eb9

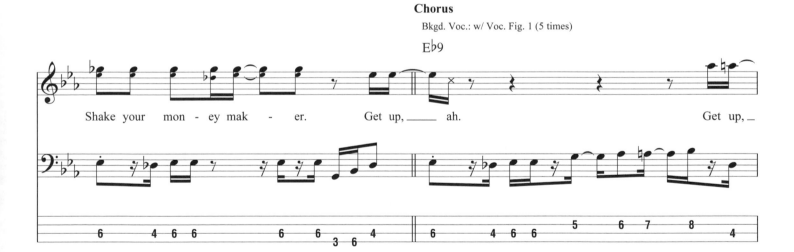

Shake your mon - ey mak - er. Get up, ___ ah. Get up, ___

___ ah. Get up, ___ ah. Get up! ___

Get up, ___ ah.

Interlude

E♭9

| 1. - 4.

| 5.

Huh!   Get up, ___

Chorus

Bkgd. Voc.: w/ Voc. Fig. 1 (3 times)

E♭9

___ ah.   Get up, ___ ah.   Get up! ___

Outro

Give It Up or Turnit A Loose

Words and Music by Charles Bobbitt

*Chord symbols reflect overall harmony.

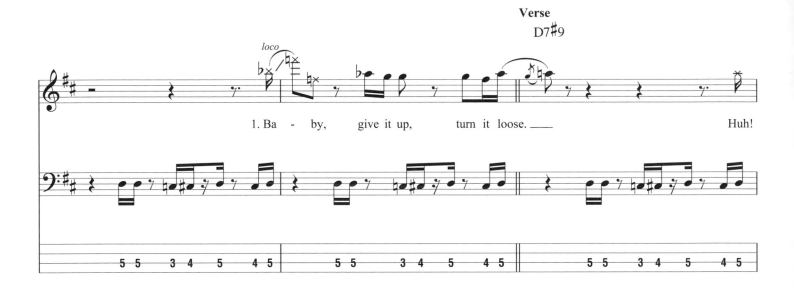

- by,   give it up   or turn it loose. _____

Start-in' o-ver a-gain.

Ba - by,   give it up   or turn it loose. _   Huh!

Ha.   Yeah, ba-

-by, give it up or turn it loose. ___ Huh!

Al-right. Yeah, ba - by, give it up, ha,

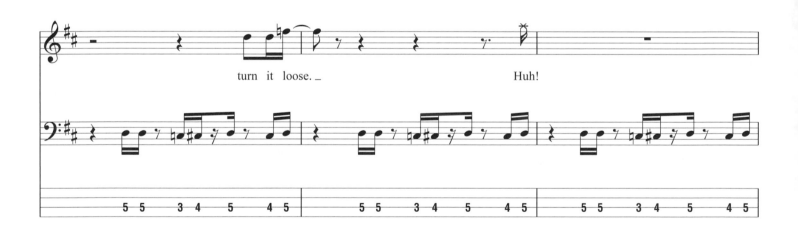

turn it loose. _ Huh!

Bridge

G9

Ah! _____ On and on. _____

Verse

D7#9

2. Yeah, ba - by, give it up, ha, uh,

turn it loose. — Lord have — mer - cy. Hey, hey, — hey, hey! —

— Uh! Ha. — Ah, —

yeah! Uh. Yeah, ba - by, need you so. —

I Got the Feelin'

Words and Music by James Brown

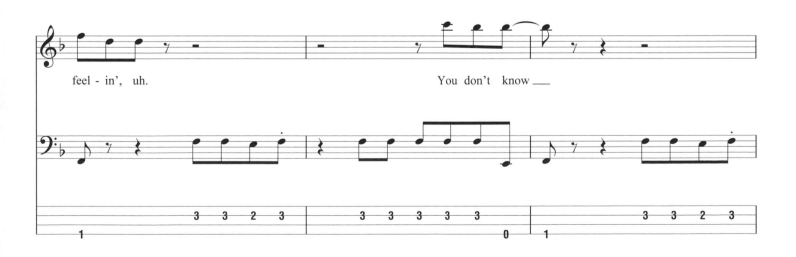

Outro-Sax Solo

Papa's Got a Brand New Bag

Words and Music by James Brown

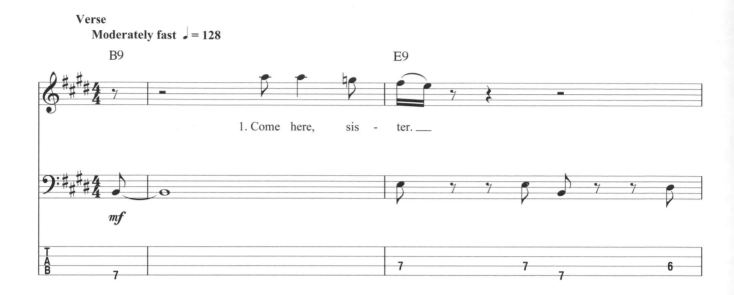

I Got You
(I Feel Good)

Words and Music by James Brown

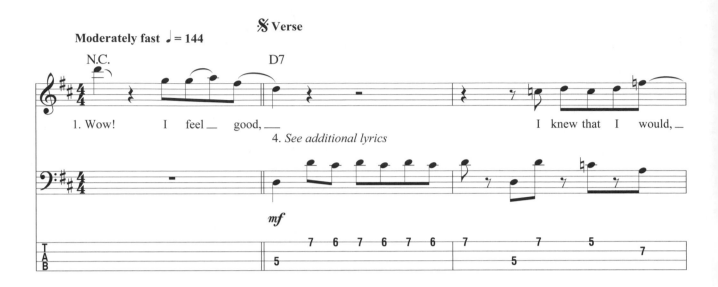

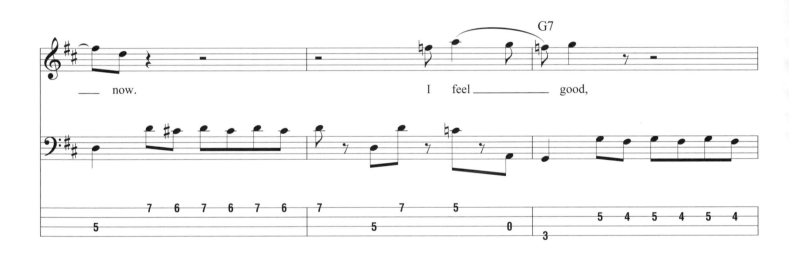

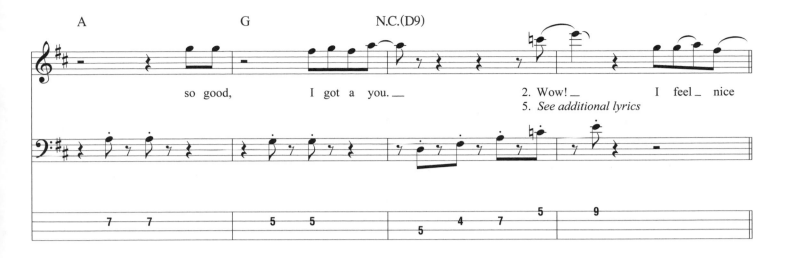

so good, I got a you. ___ 2. Wow! ___ I feel ___ nice
5. *See additional lyrics*

Verse

___ 2., 3. like sug - ar and spice. _____

I feel _____ nice, like sug - ar and spice. ___

So nice, so nice,

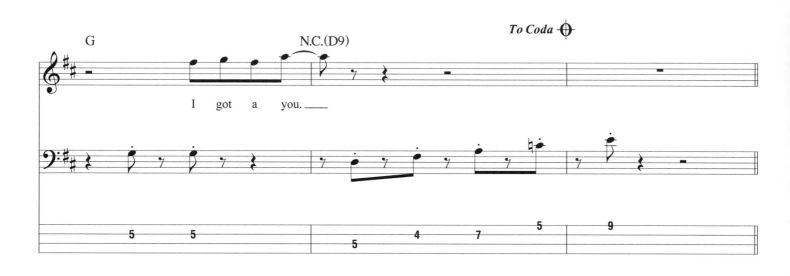

I got a you. ____

To Coda ⊕

Interlude

When I

Bridge

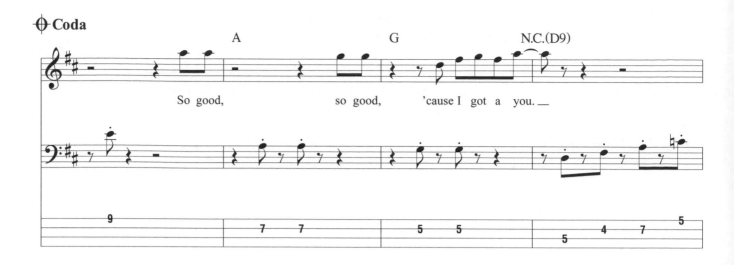

So good, so good, 'cause I got a you.

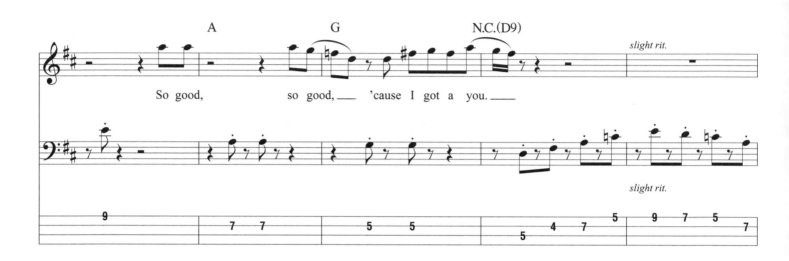

So good, so good, 'cause I got a you.

slight rit.

Free time

Hey! Ah, oo.

Additional Lyrics

4. And I feel nice,
   Like sugar and spice.
   I feel nice,
   Like sugar and spice.
   So nice, so nice
   That I got a you.

5. Wow! I feel good,
   I knew that I would, now.
   I feel good,
   I knew that I would.
   So good, so good
   That I got a you.

HAL•LEONARD BASS PLAY-ALONG

 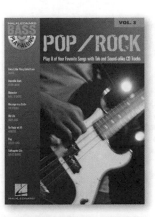 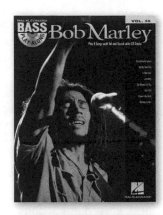

 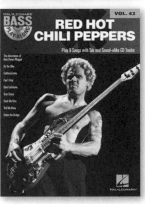 

The Bass Play-Along™ Series will help you play your favorite songs quickly and easily! Just follow the tab, listen to the CD or online audio to hear how the bass should sound, and then play along using the separate backing tracks. The melody and lyrics are also included in the book in case you want to sing, or to simply help you follow along. The audio files are enhanced so you can adjust the recording to any tempo without changing pitch!

1. Rock
00699674 Book/CD Pack.................................$12.95

2. R&B
00699675 Book/CD Pack.................................$14.99

3. Pop/Rock
00699677 Book/CD Pack.................................$12.95

4. '90s Rock
00699679 Book/CD Pack.................................$12.95

5. Funk
00699680 Book/CD Pack.................................$12.95

6. Classic Rock
00699678 Book/CD Pack.................................$12.95

7. Hard Rock
00699676 Book/CD Pack.................................$14.95

9. Blues
00699817 Book/CD Pack.................................$14.99

10. Jimi Hendrix Smash Hits
00699815 Book/CD Pack.................................$17.99

11. Country
00699818 Book/CD Pack.................................$12.95

12. Punk Classics
00699814 Book/CD Pack.................................$12.99

13. Lennon & McCartney
00699816 Book/CD Pack.................................$14.99

14. Modern Rock
00699821 Book/CD Pack.................................$14.99

15. Mainstream Rock
00699822 Book/CD Pack.................................$14.99

16. '80s Metal
00699825 Book/CD Pack.................................$16.99

17. Pop Metal
00699826 Book/CD Pack.................................$14.99

18. Blues Rock
00699828 Book/CD Pack.................................$14.99

19. Steely Dan
00700203 Book/CD Pack.................................$16.99

20. The Police
00700270 Book/CD Pack.................................$14.99

21. Rock Band – Modern Rock
00700705 Book/CD Pack.................................$14.95

22. Rock Band – Classic Rock
00700706 Book/CD Pack.................................$14.95

**23. Pink Floyd –
Dark Side of The Moon**
00700847 Book/CD Pack.................................$14.99

24. Weezer
00700960 Book/CD Pack.................................$14.99

25. Nirvana
00701047 Book/CD Pack.................................$14.99

26. Black Sabbath
00701180 Book/CD Pack.................................$16.99

27. Kiss
00701181 Book/CD Pack.................................$14.99

28. The Who
00701182 Book/CD Pack.................................$14.99

29. Eric Clapton
00701183 Book/CD Pack.................................$14.99

30. Early Rock
00701184 Book/CD Pack.................................$15.99

31. The 1970s
00701185 Book/CD Pack.................................$14.99

32. Disco
00701186 Book/CD Pack.................................$14.99

33. Christmas Hits
00701197 Book/CD Pack.................................$12.99

34. Easy Songs
00701480 Book/CD Pack.................................$12.99

35. Bob Marley
00701702 Book/CD Pack.................................$14.99

36. Aerosmith
00701886 Book/CD Pack.................................$14.99

37. Modern Worship
00701920 Book/CD Pack.................................$12.99

38. Avenged Sevenfold
00702386 Book/CD Pack.................................$16.99

40. AC/DC
14041594 Book/CD Pack.................................$16.99

41. U2
00702582 Book/CD Pack.................................$16.99

42. Red Hot Chili Peppers
00702991 Book/CD Pack.................................$19.99

43. Paul McCartney
00703079 Book/CD Pack.................................$17.99

44. Megadeth
00703080 Book/CD Pack.................................$16.99

45. Slipknot
00703201 Book/CD Pack.................................$16.99

46. Best Bass Lines Ever
00103359 Book/Online Audio......................$17.99

48. James Brown
00117421 Book/CD Pack.................................$16.99

49. Eagles
00119936 Book/CD Pack.................................$17.99

FOR MORE INFORMATION, SEE YOUR LOCAL MUSIC DEALER,
OR WRITE TO:

HAL•LEONARD® CORPORATION
7777 W. BLUEMOUND RD. P.O. BOX 13819 MILWAUKEE, WI 53213

Prices, contents, and availability subject to change without notice.

Visit Hal Leonard Online at **www.halleonard.com**

BASS RECORDED VERSIONS

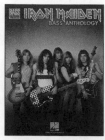  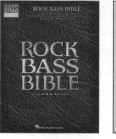

  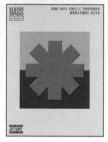

Bass Recorded Versions
feature authentic transcriptions
written in standard notation
and tablature for bass guitar.
This series features complete
bass lines from the classics
to contemporary superstars.

25 All-Time Rock Bass Classics
00690445 / $14.95

25 Essential Rock Bass Classics
00690210 / $15.95

Avenged Sevenfold – Nightmare
00691054 / $19.99

Best of Victor Bailey
00690718 / $19.95

Bass Tab 1990-1999
00690400 / $16.95

Bass Tab 1999-2000
00690404 / $14.95

Bass Tab 2013
00121899 / $19.99

Bass Tab White Pages
00690508 / $29.99

The Beatles Bass Lines
00690170 / $14.95

The Beatles 1962-1966
00690556 / $18.99

The Beatles 1967-1970
00690557 / $19.99

The Best of Blink 182
00690549 / $18.95

Blues Bass Classics
00690291 / $14.95

Boston Bass Collection
00690935 / $19.95

The Best of Eric Clapton
00660187 / $19.95

Stanley Clarke Collection
00672307 / $19.95

Funk Bass Bible
00690744 / $19.95

Hard Rock Bass Bible
00690746 / $17.95

**Jimi Hendrix –
Are You Experienced?**
00690371 / $17.95

Incubus – Morning View
00690639 / $17.95

Iron Maiden Bass Anthology
00690867 / $22.99

Jazz Bass Classics
00102070 / $17.99

Best of Kiss for Bass
00690080 / $19.95

**Lynyrd Skynyrd –
All-Time Greatest Hits**
00690956 / $19.99

Bob Marley Bass Collection
00690568 / $19.95

Mastodon – Crack the Skye
00691007 / $19.99

Megadeth Bass Anthology
00691191 / $19.99

Metal Bass Tabs
00103358 / $19.99

Best of Marcus Miller
00690811 / $24.99

Motown Bass Classics
00690253 / $14.95

Muse Bass Tab Collection
00123275 / $19.99

Nirvana Bass Collection
00690066 / $19.95

No Doubt – Tragic Kingdom
00120112 / $22.95

The Offspring – Greatest Hits
00690809 / $17.95

**Jaco Pastorius –
Greatest Jazz Fusion Bass Player**
00690421 / $19.99

The Essential Jaco Pastorius
00690420 / $19.99

Pearl Jam – Ten
00694882 / $16.99

Pink Floyd – Dark Side of the Moon
00660172 / $14.95

The Best of Police
00660207 / $14.95

Pop/Rock Bass Bible
00690747 / $17.95

Queen – The Bass Collection
00690065 / $19.99

R&B Bass Bible
00690745 / $17.95

Rage Against the Machine
00690248 / $17.99

The Best of Red Hot Chili Peppers
00695285 / $24.95

**Red Hot Chili Peppers –
Blood Sugar Sex Magik**
00690064 / $19.95

Red Hot Chili Peppers – By the Way
00690585 / $19.95

**Red Hot Chili Peppers –
Californication**
00690390 / $19.95

**Red Hot Chili Peppers –
Greatest Hits**
00690675 / $18.95

**Red Hot Chili Peppers –
I'm with You**
00691167 / $22.99

**Red Hot Chili Peppers –
One Hot Minute**
00690091 / $18.95

**Red Hot Chili Peppers –
Stadium Arcadium**
00690853 / $24.95

**Red Hot Chili Peppers –
Stadium Arcadium: Deluxe Edition**
Book/2-CD Pack
00690863 / $39.95

Rock Bass Bible
00690446 / $19.95

Rolling Stones
00690256 / $16.95

**Stevie Ray Vaughan –
Lightnin' Blues 1983-1987**
00694778 / $19.95

Best of Yes
00103044 / $19.99

Best of ZZ Top for Bass
00691069 / $22.99